I0467587

Meaningful Celestial Tattoo Drawings

Draw Celestial Tattoos With Meaning

Celestial Tattoos

By : Gala Publication

2

Published By :

Gala Publication
© Copyright 2015 – Gala Publication

ISBN-13: **978-1522707523**
ISBN-10: **1522707522**

Table of Contents

EARTH TATTOO

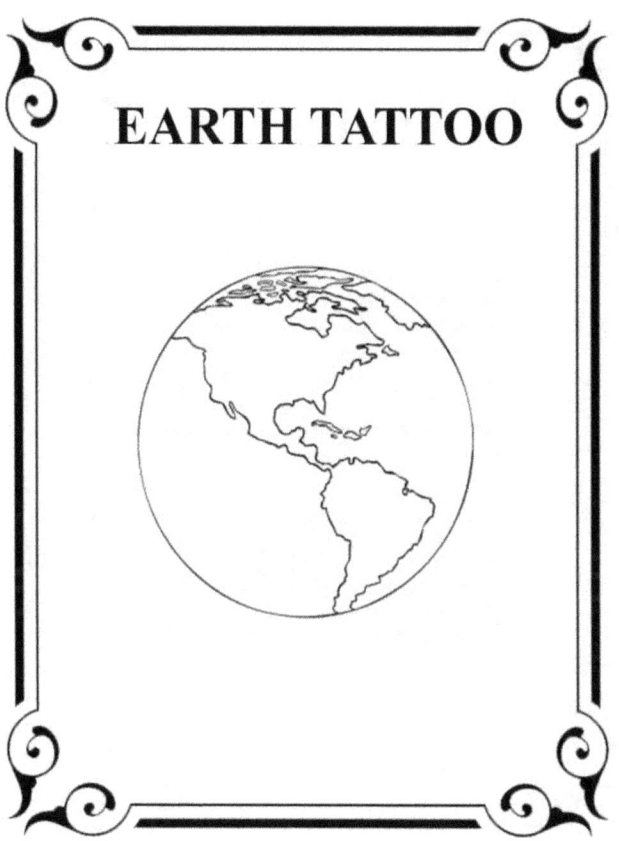

STEP 1

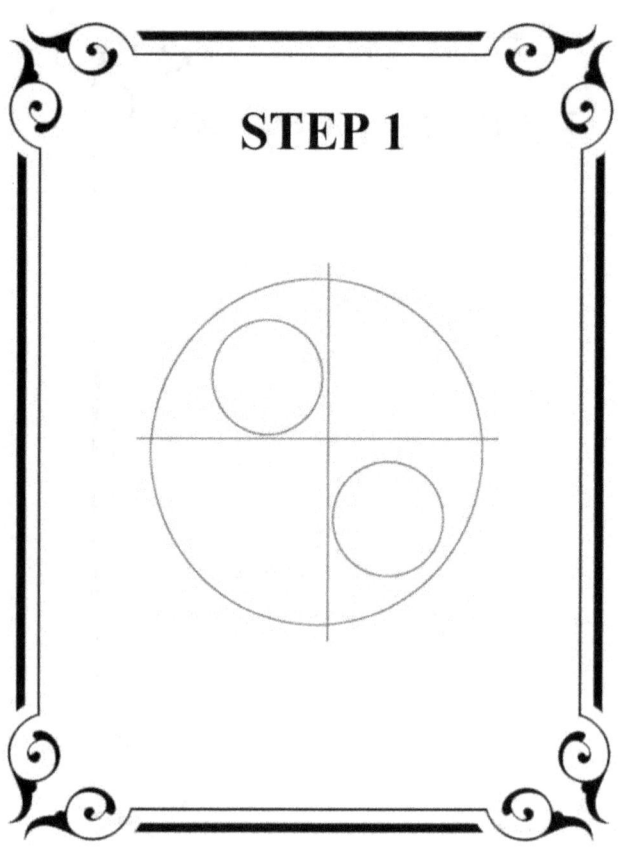

STEP 2

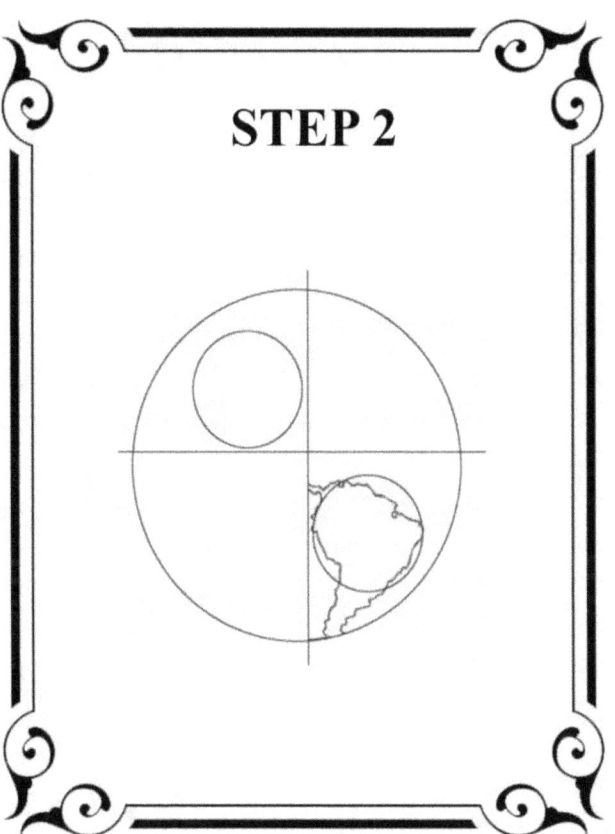

STEP 3

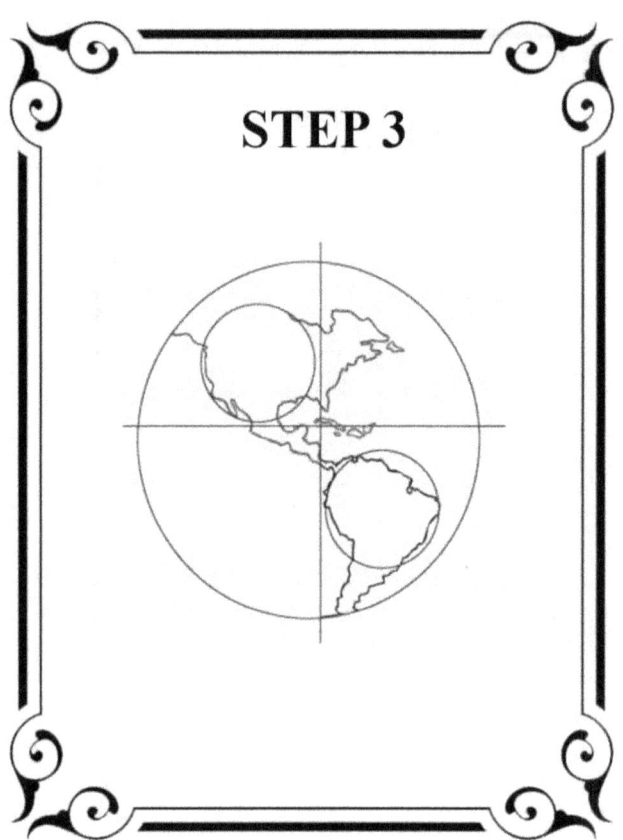

STEP 4

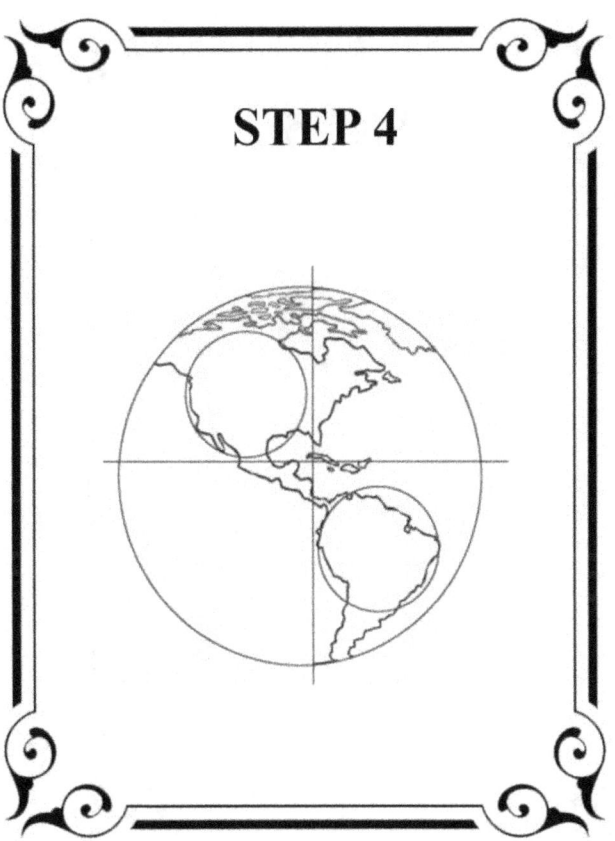

STEP 5

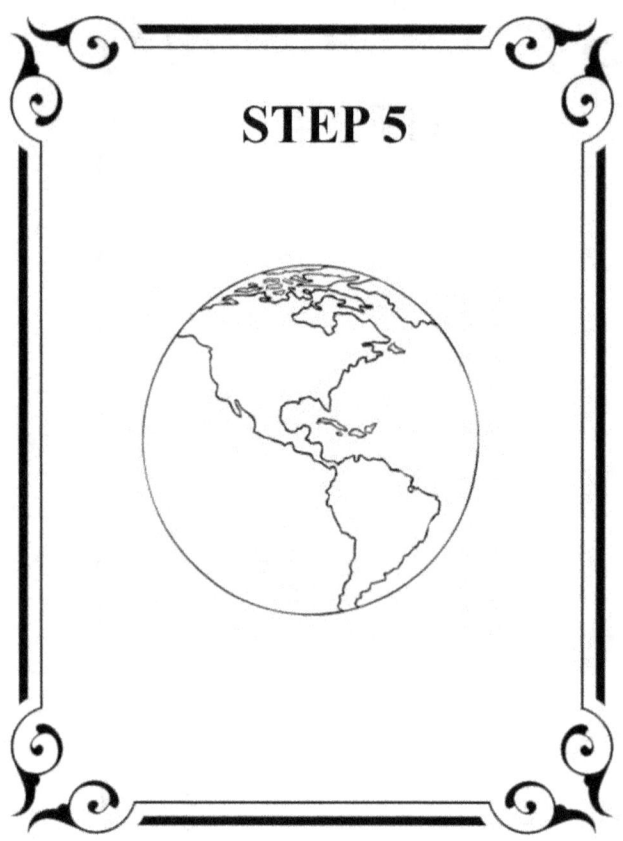

MARS TATTOO

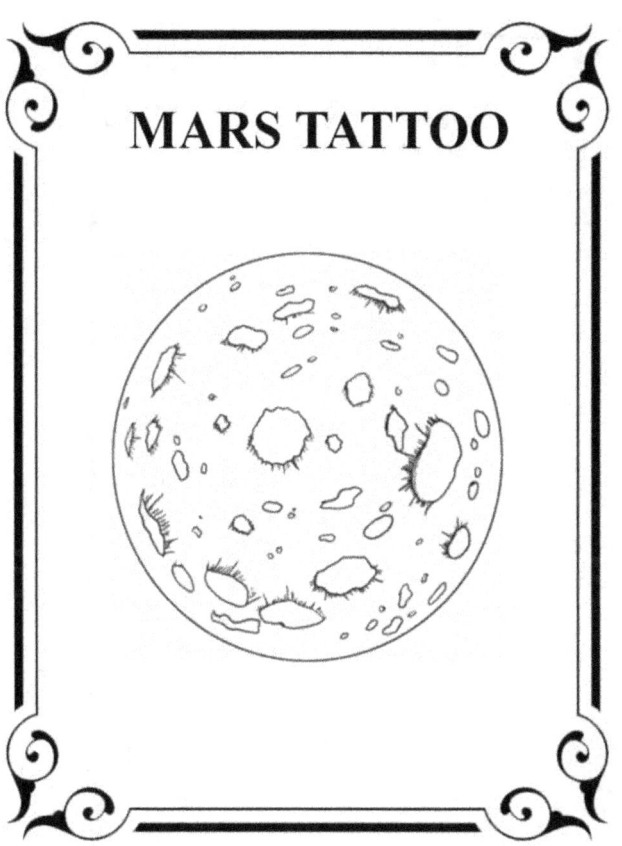

STEP 1

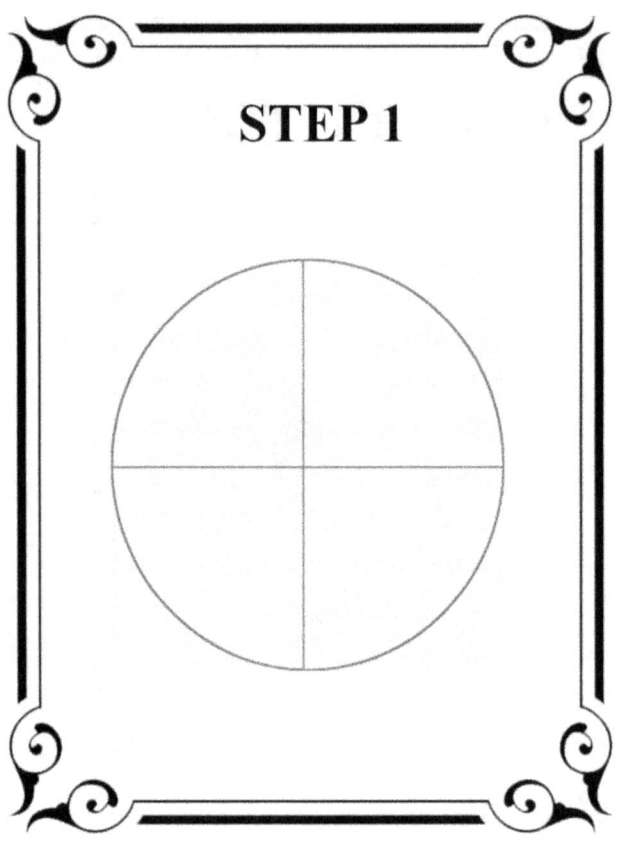

STEP 2

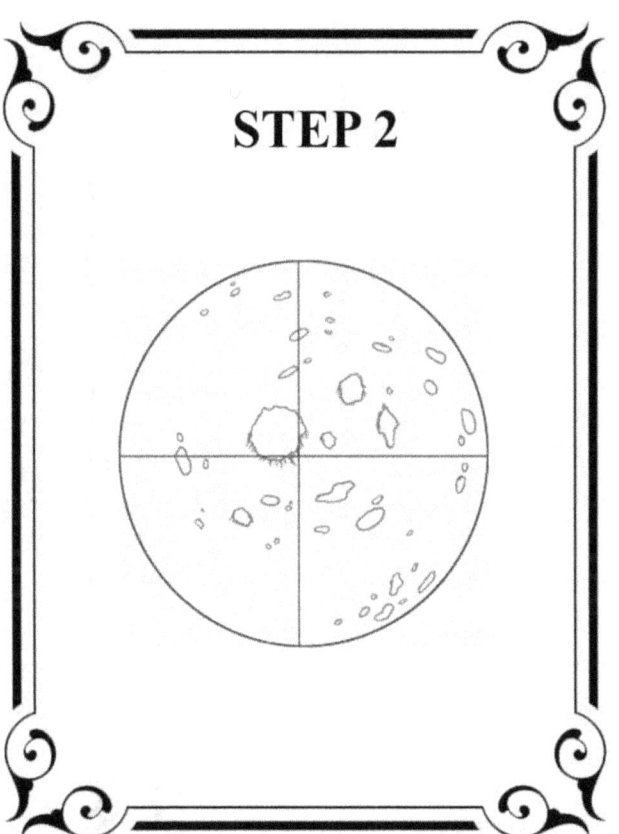

STEP 3

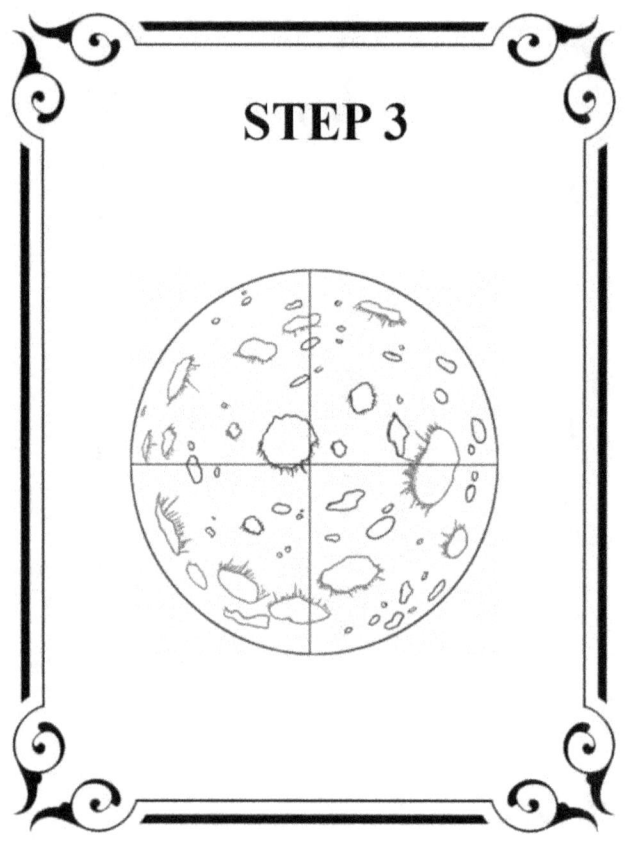

STEP 4

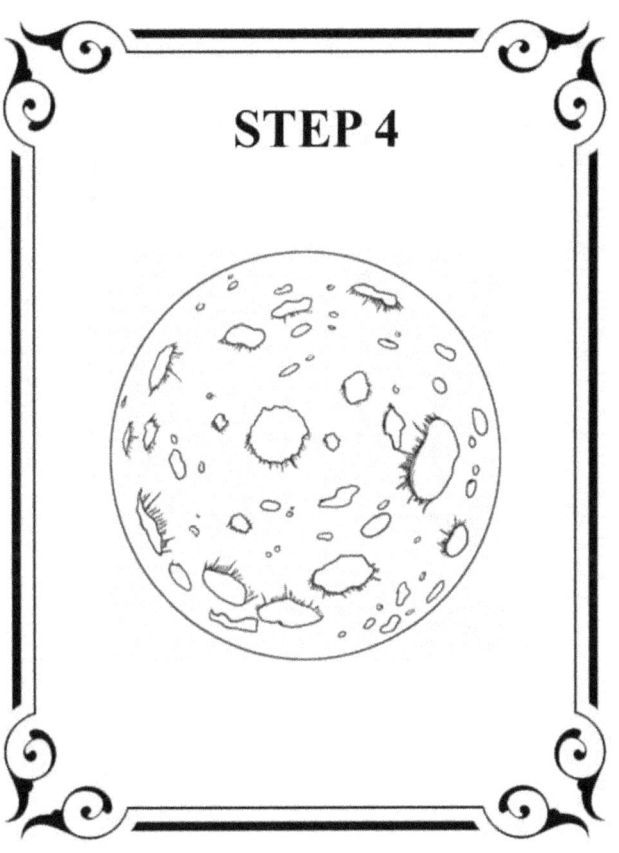

MOON TATTOO

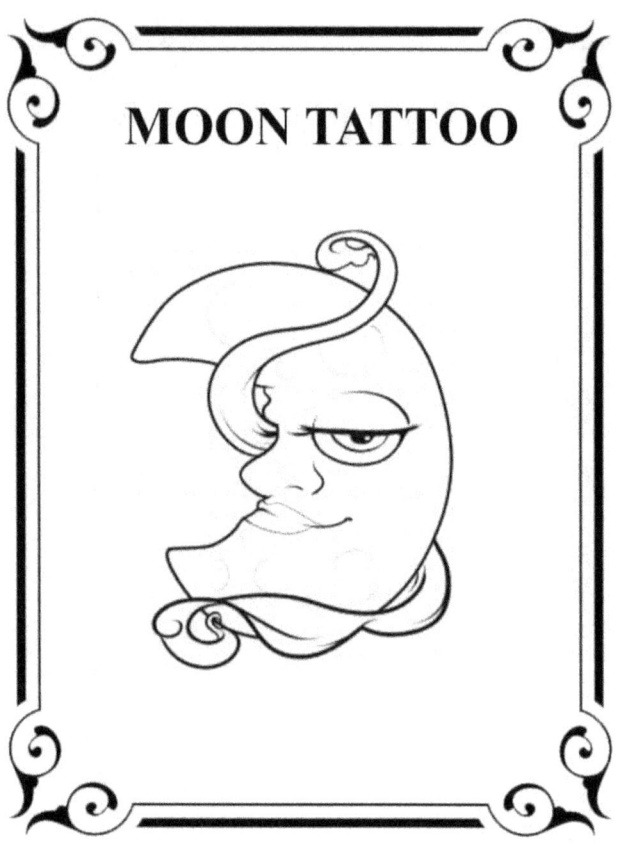

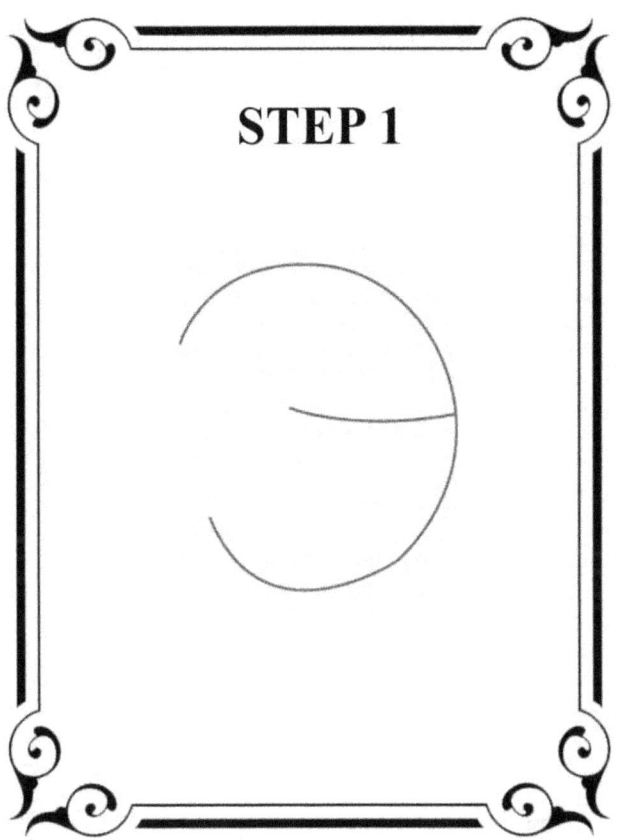

STEP 1

STEP 2

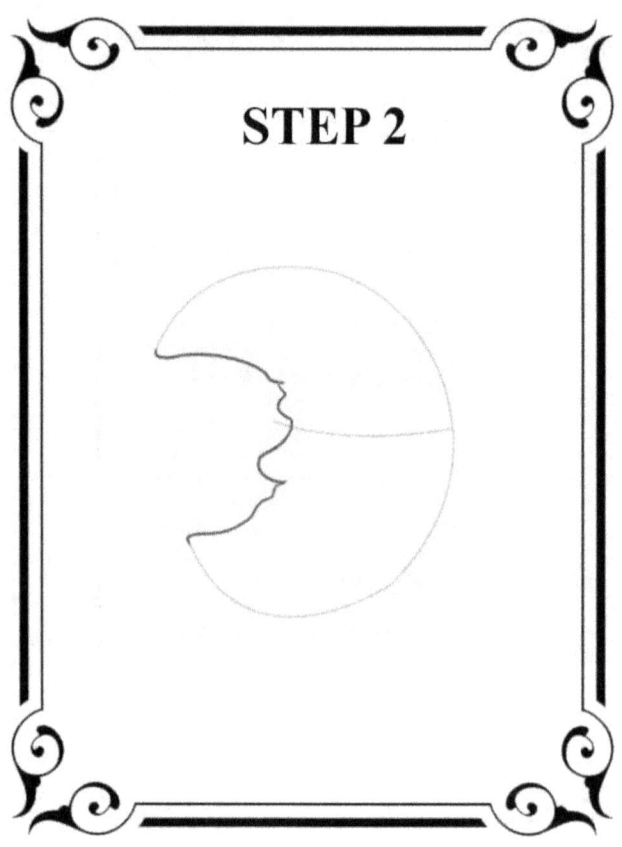

STEP 3

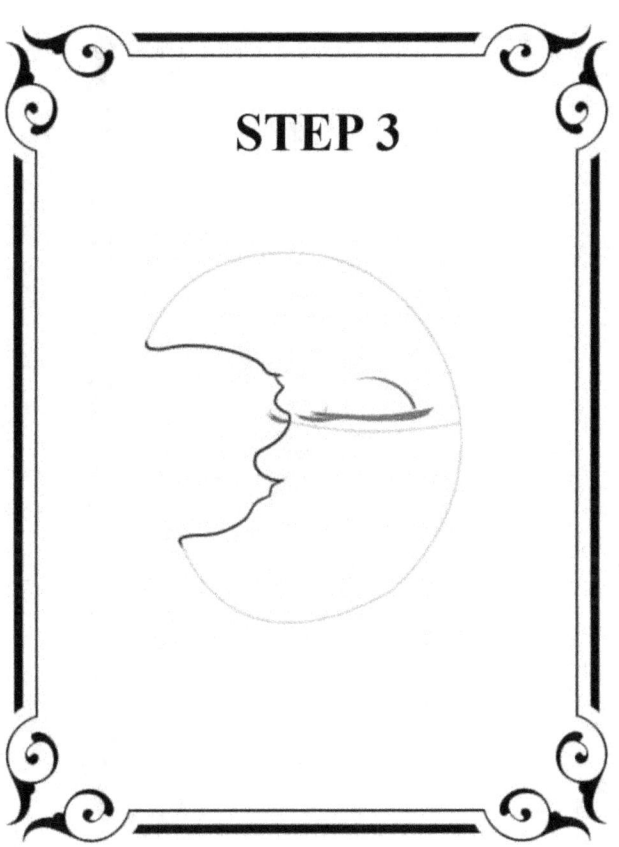

STEP 4

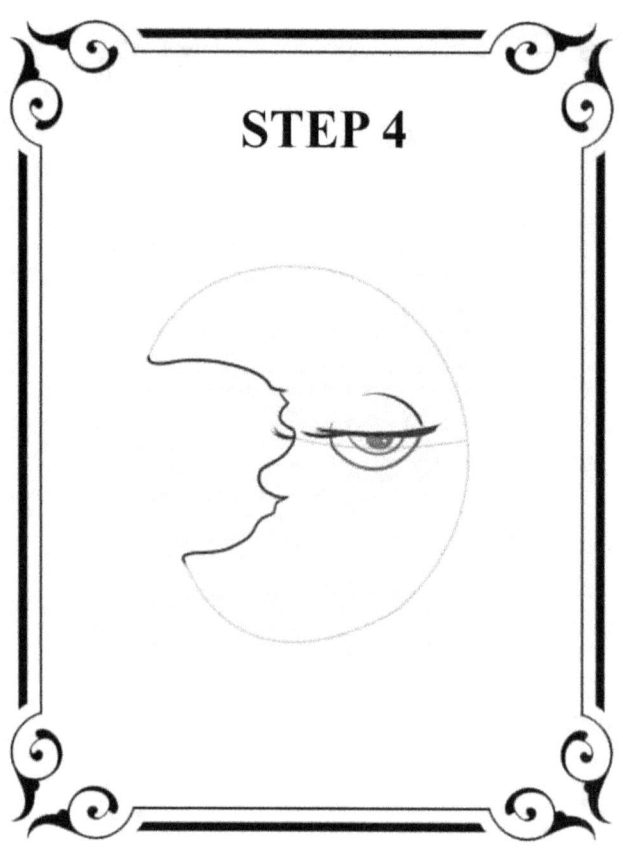

STEP 5

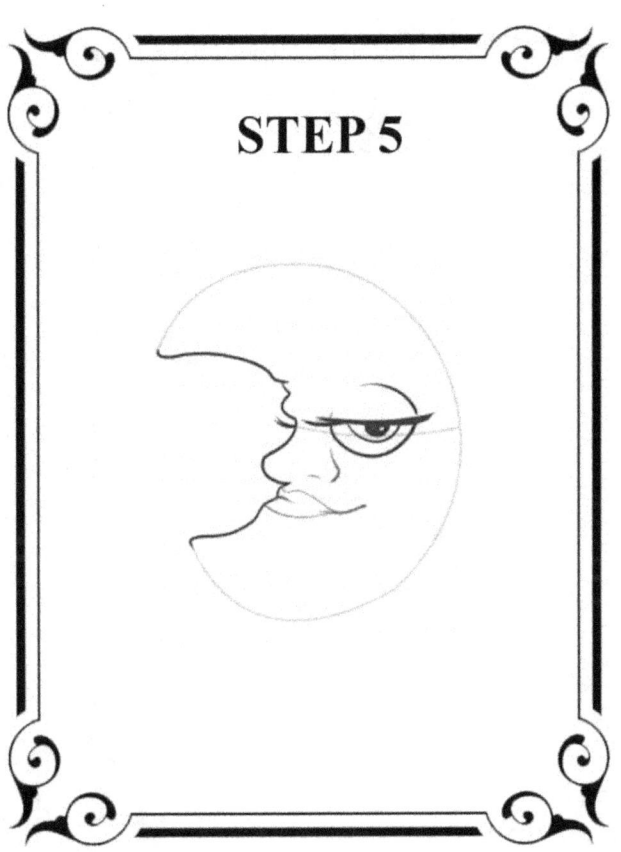

STEP 6

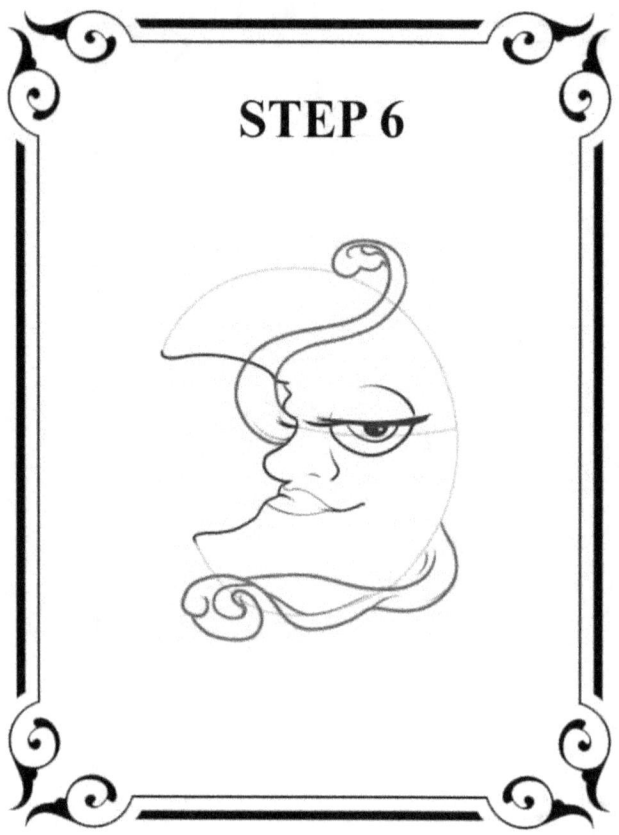

STEP 7

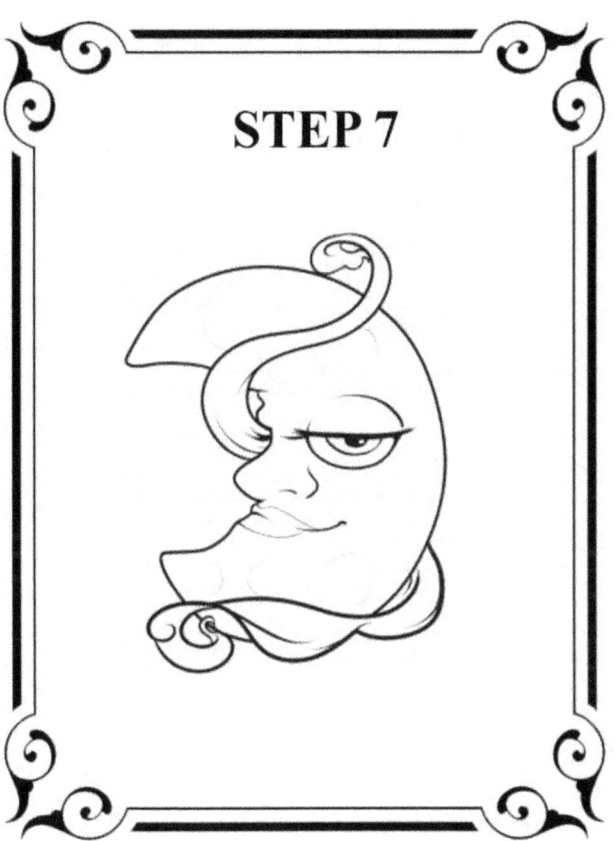

PLANET TATTOO

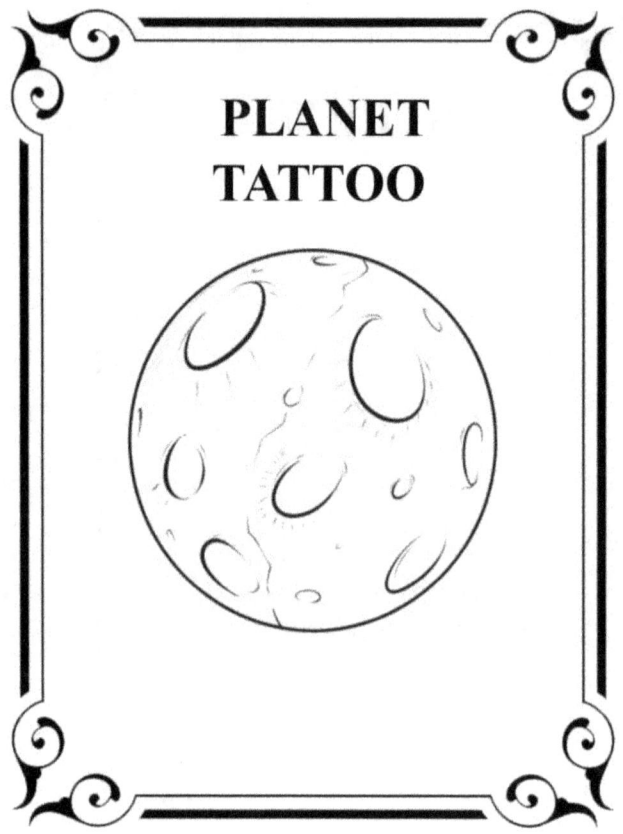

STEP 1

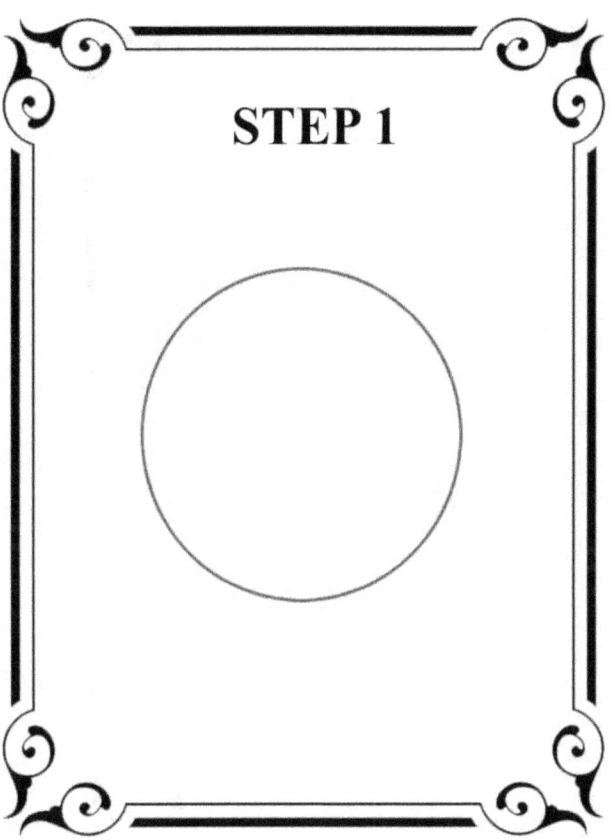

STEP 2

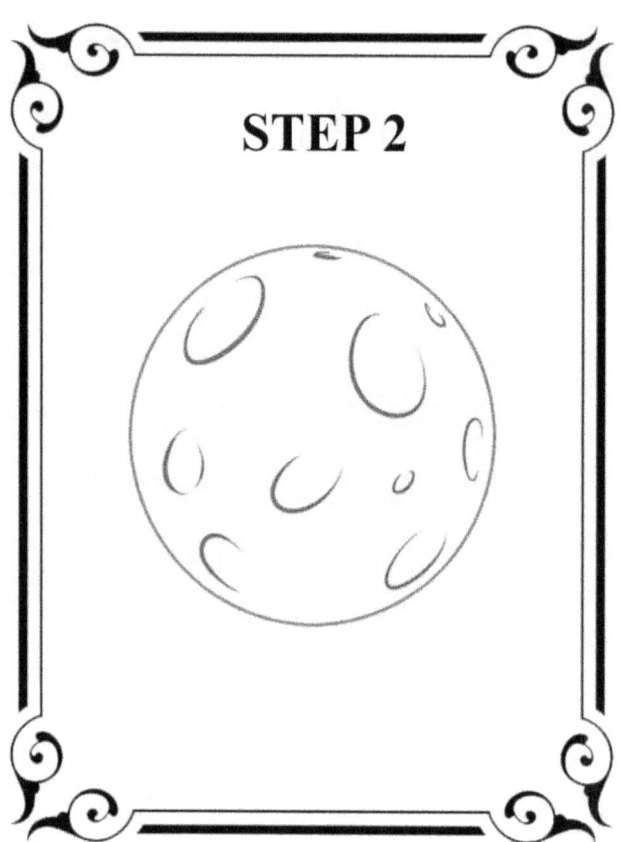

STEP 3

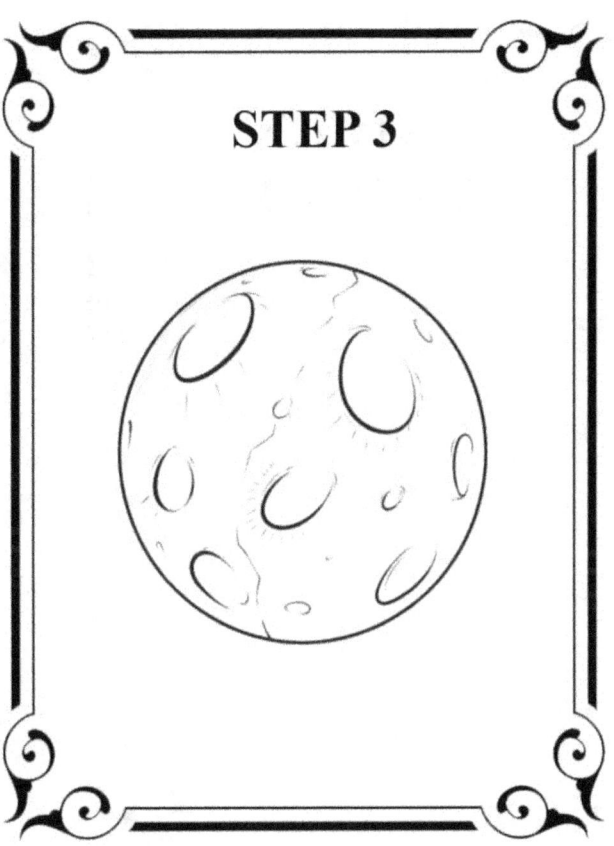

SATURN
TATTOO

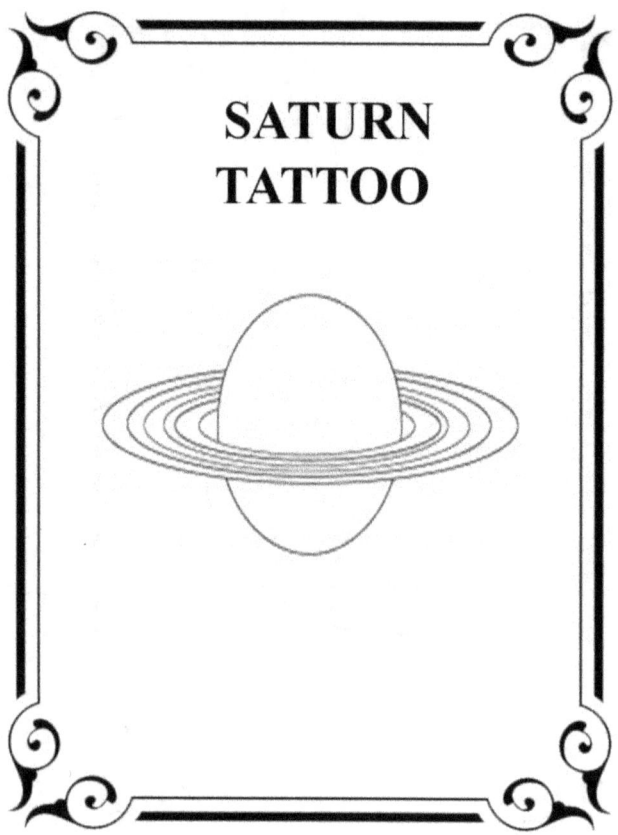

STEP 1

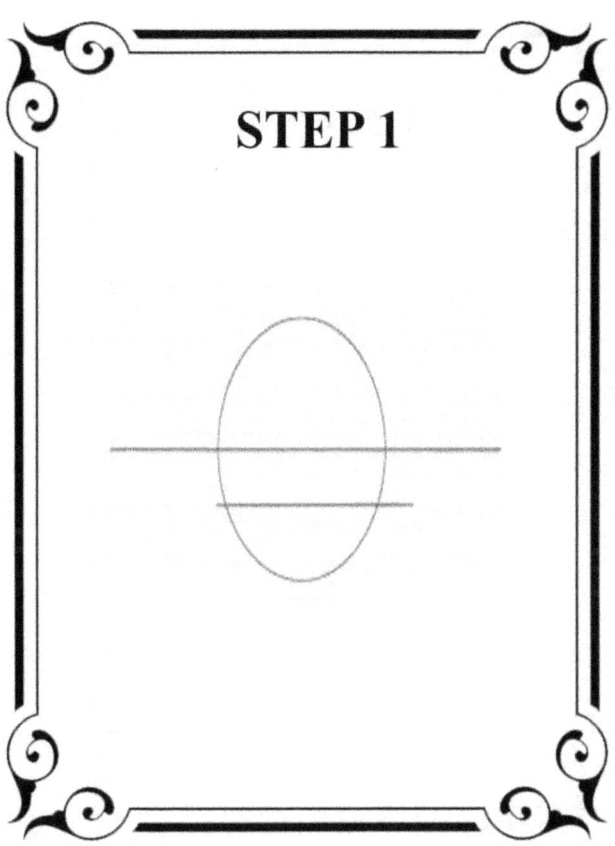

STEP 2

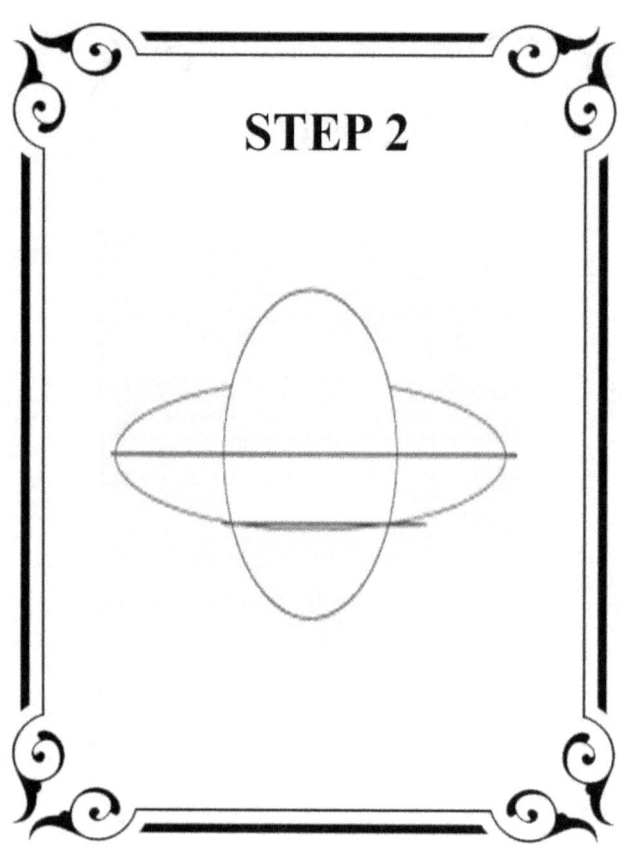

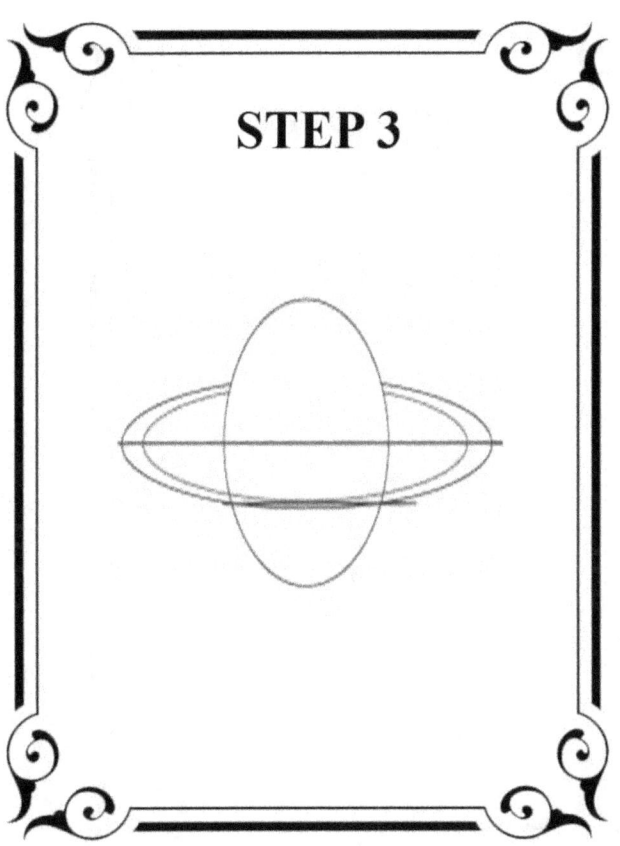

STEP 3

STEP 4

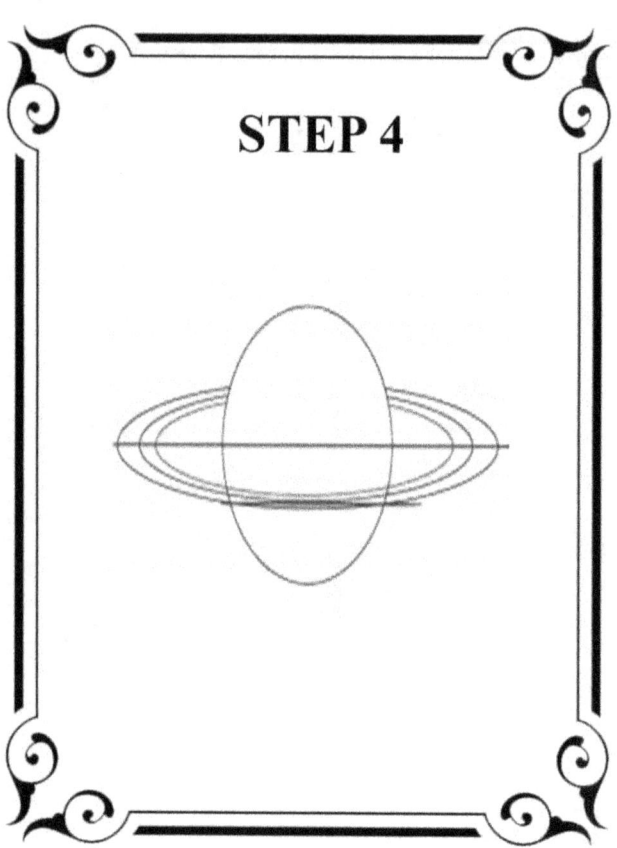

STEP 5

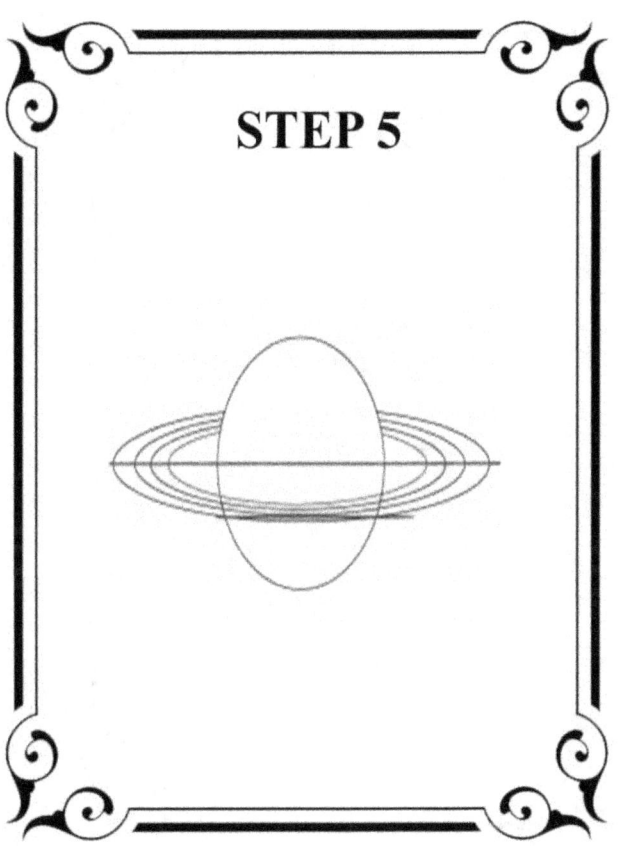

STEP 5

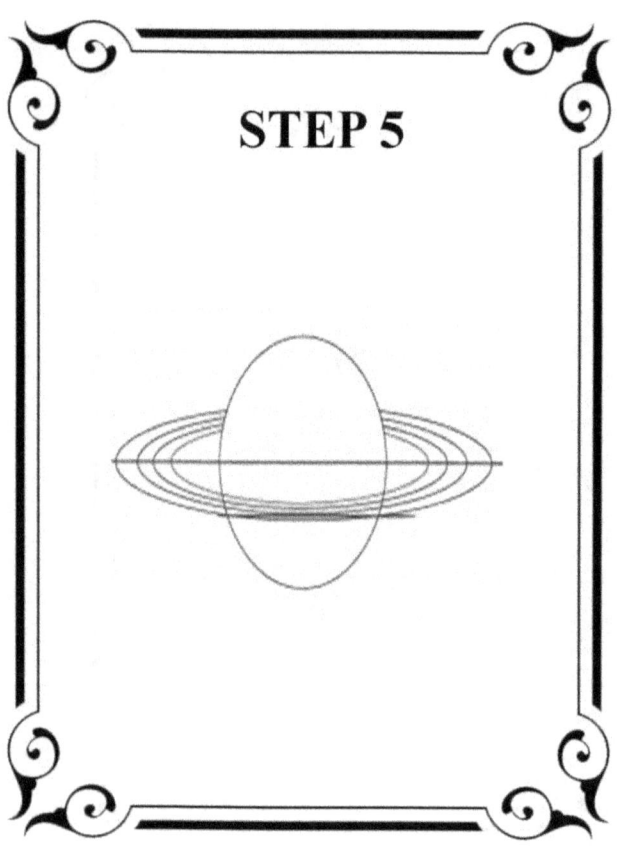

STEP 6

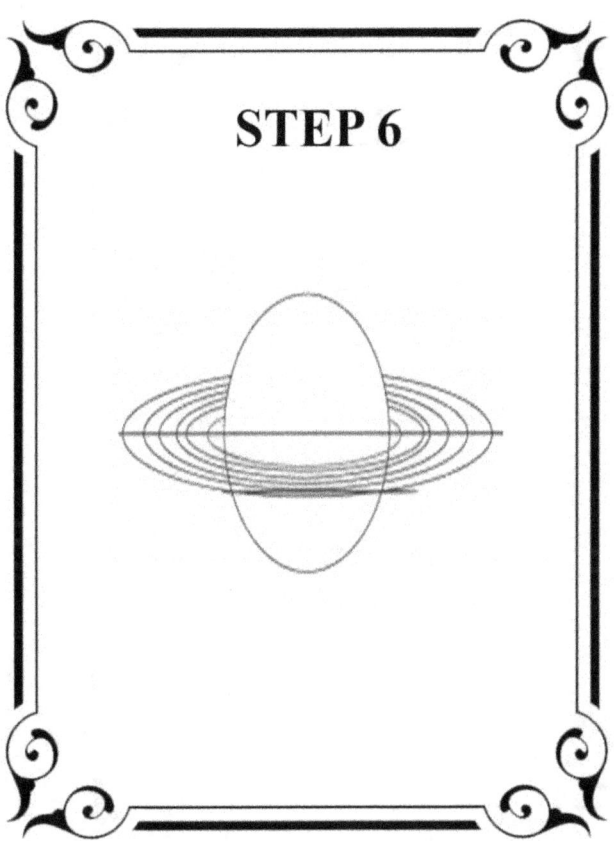

STEP 7

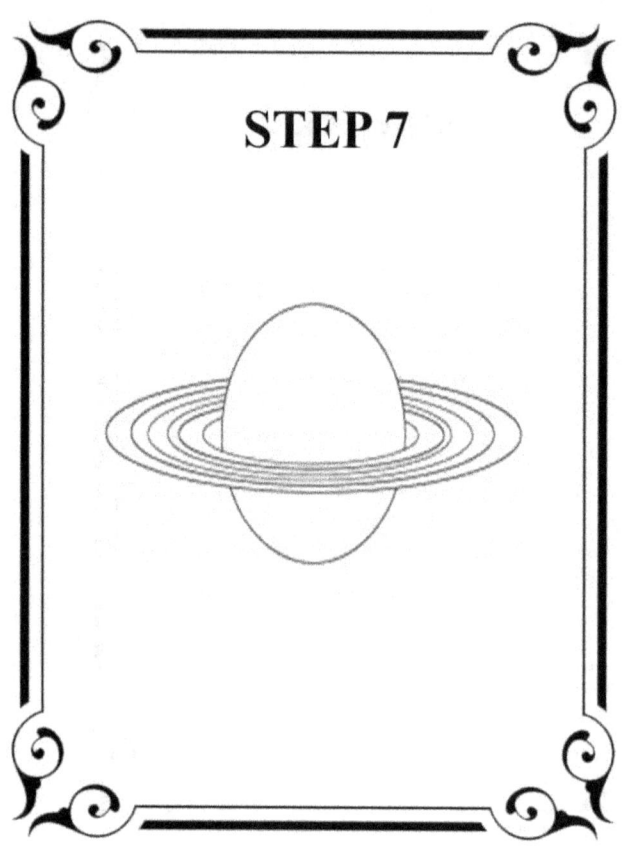

STAR TATTOO

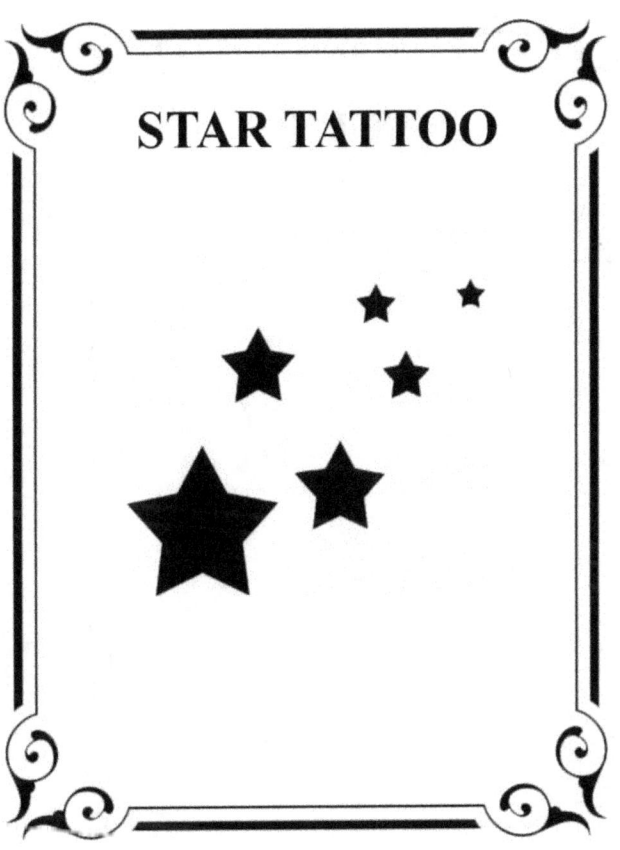

STEP 1

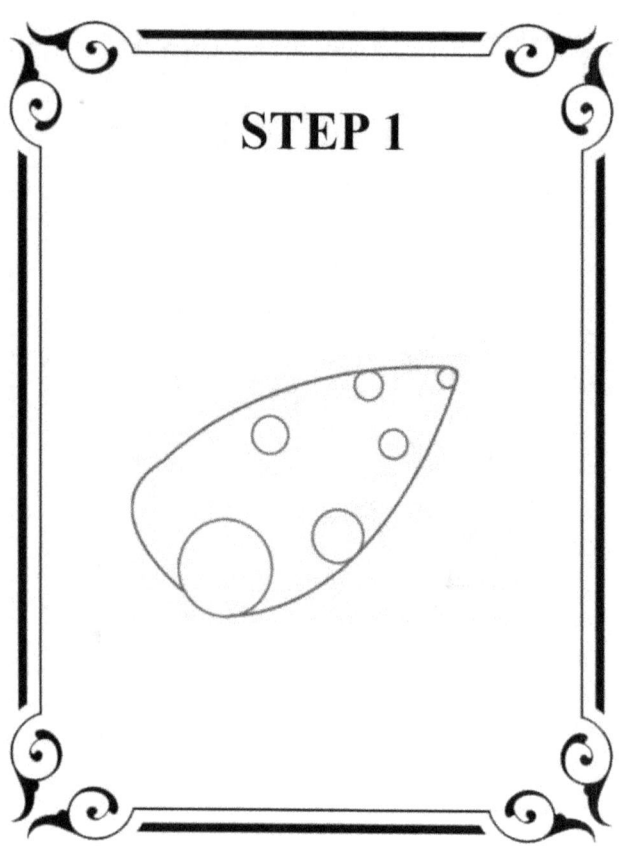

STEP 2

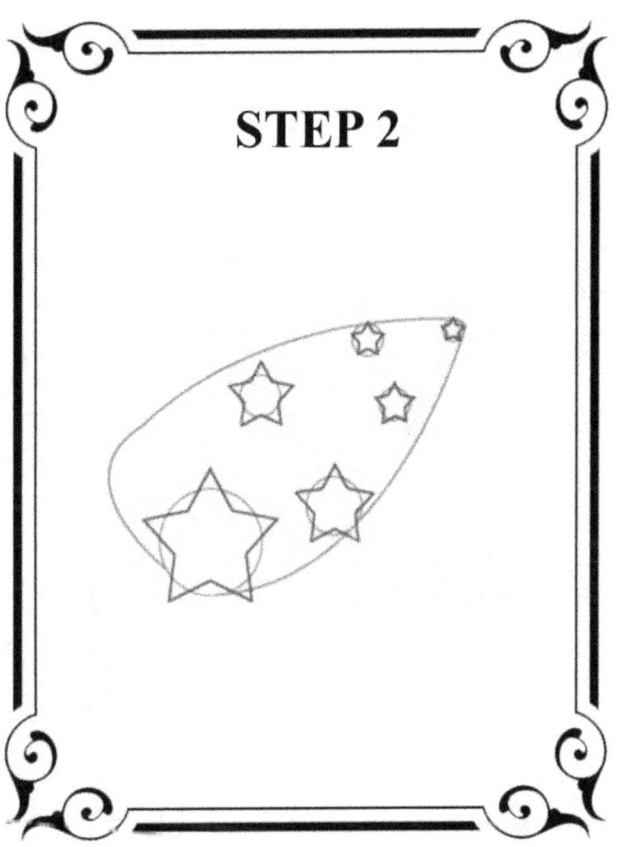

STEP 3

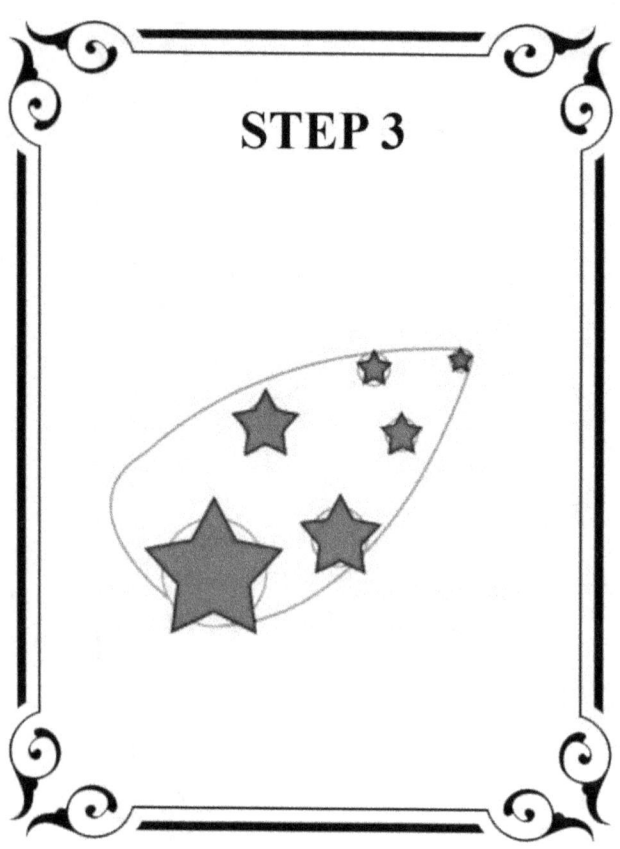

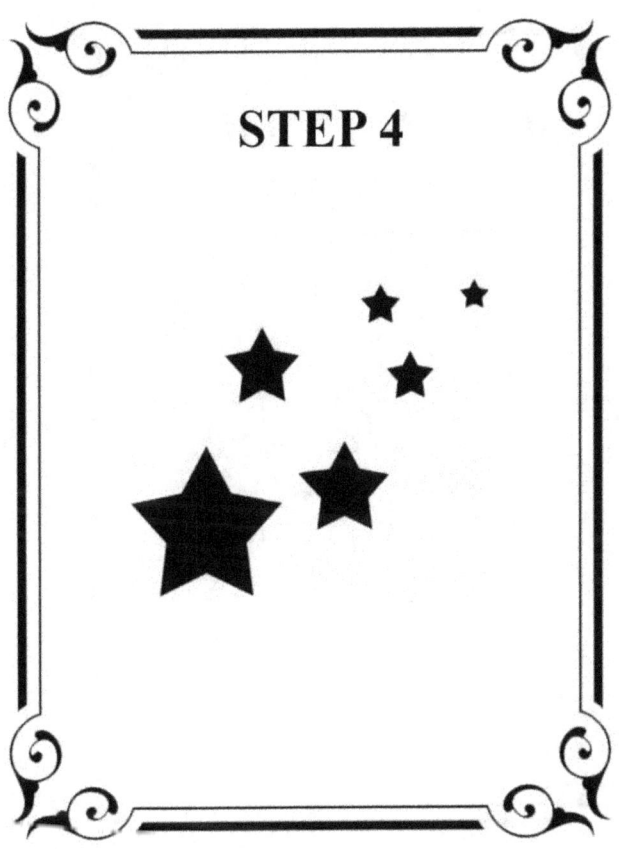

STEP 4

SUN AND MOON TATTOO

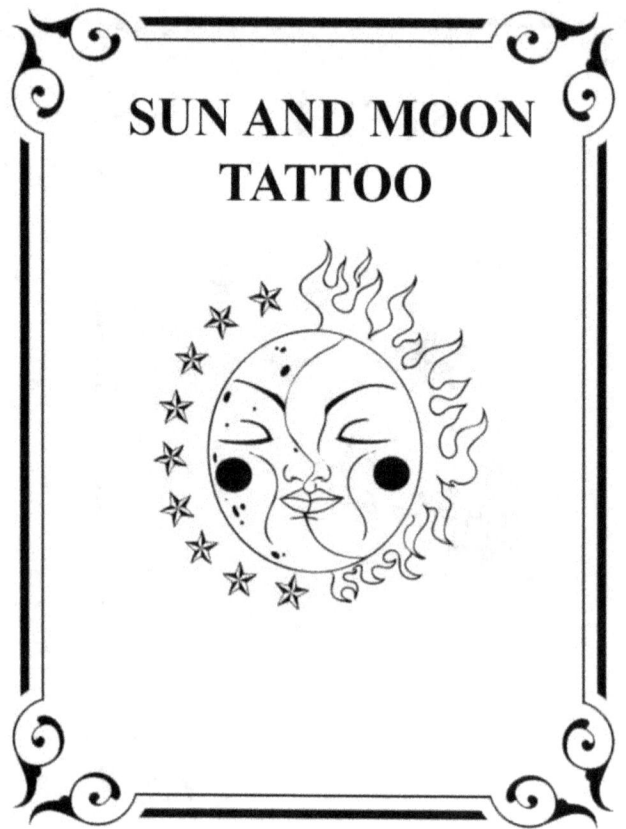

STEP 1

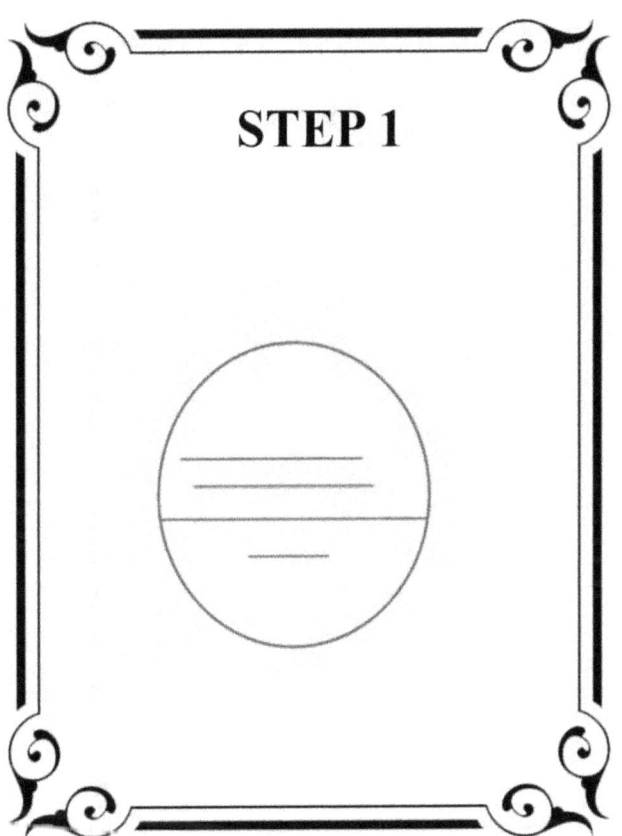

STEP 2

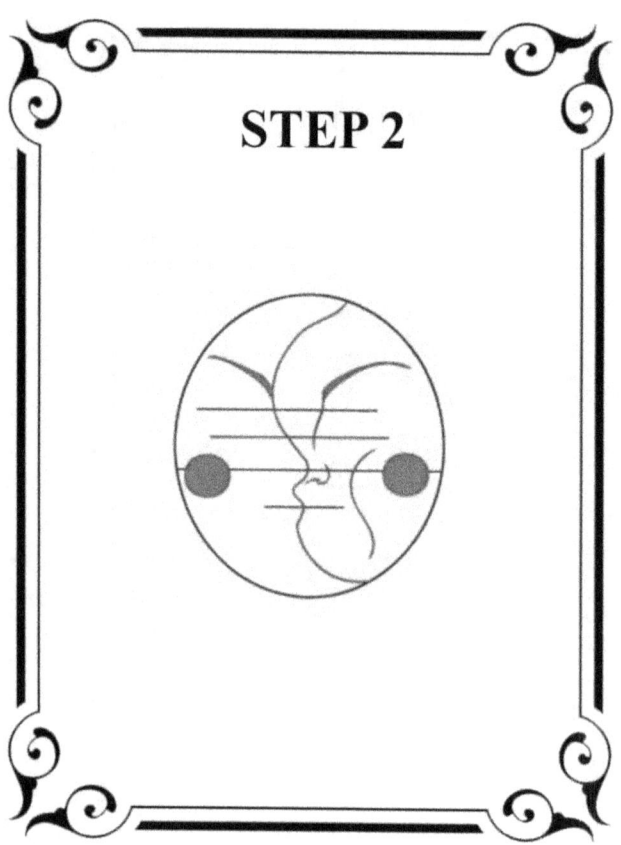

STEP 3

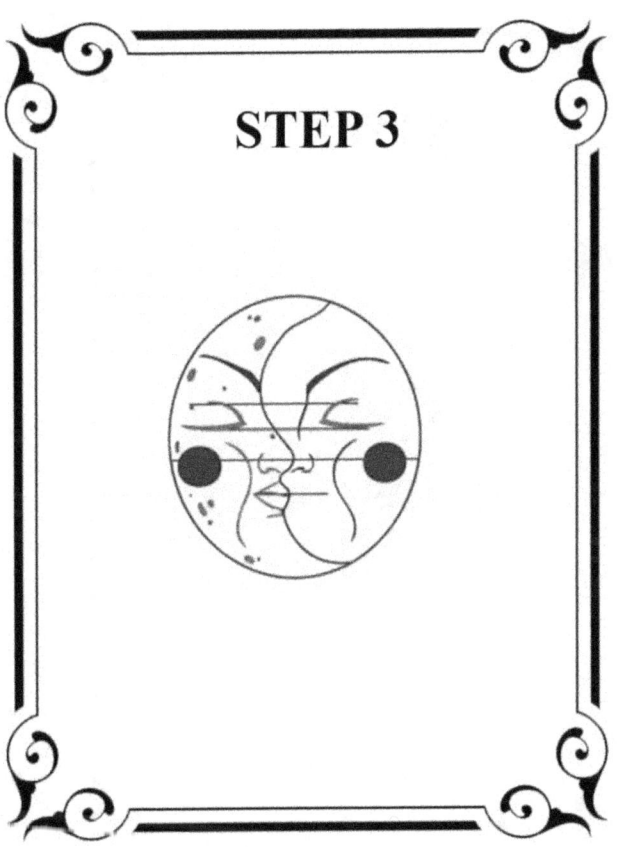

STEP 4

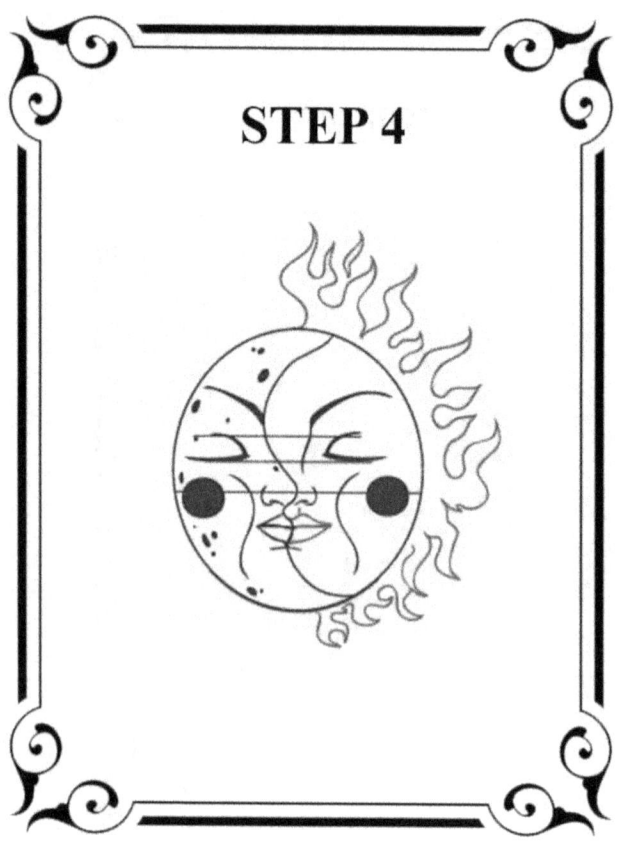

STEP 5

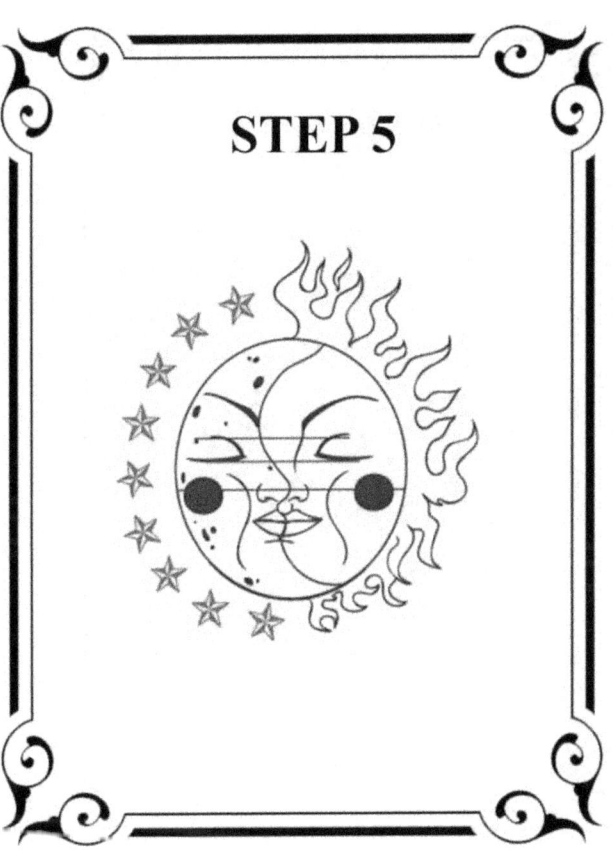

STEP 6

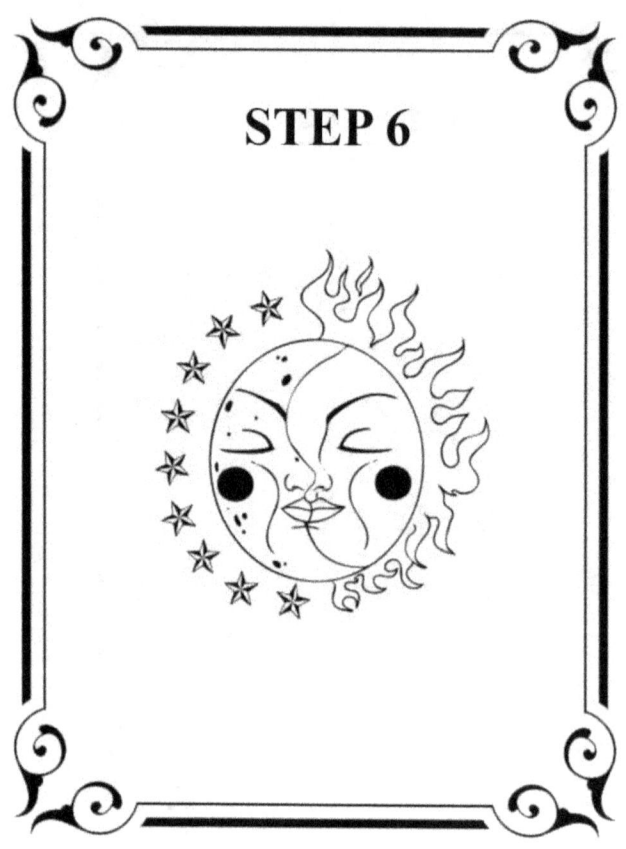

SUN TATTOO

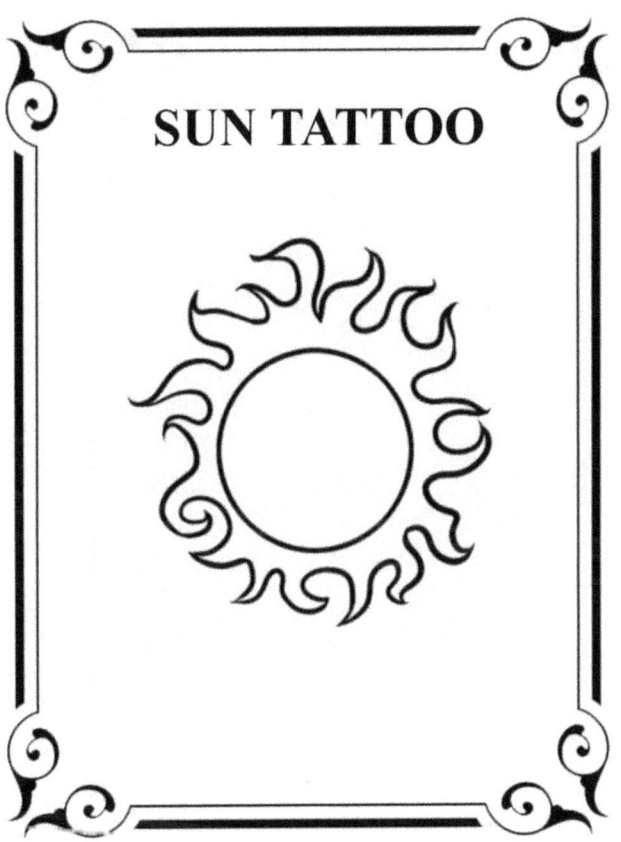

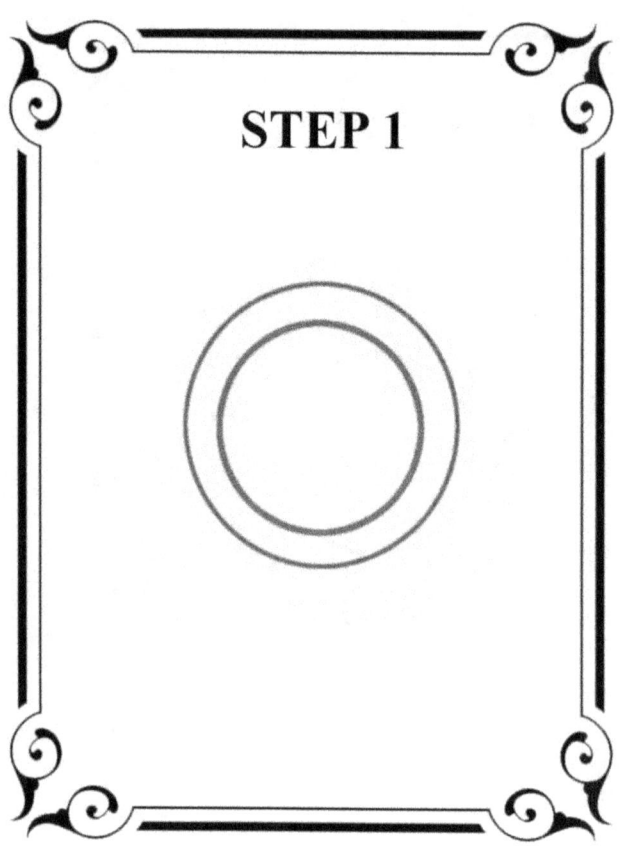

STEP 1

STEP 2

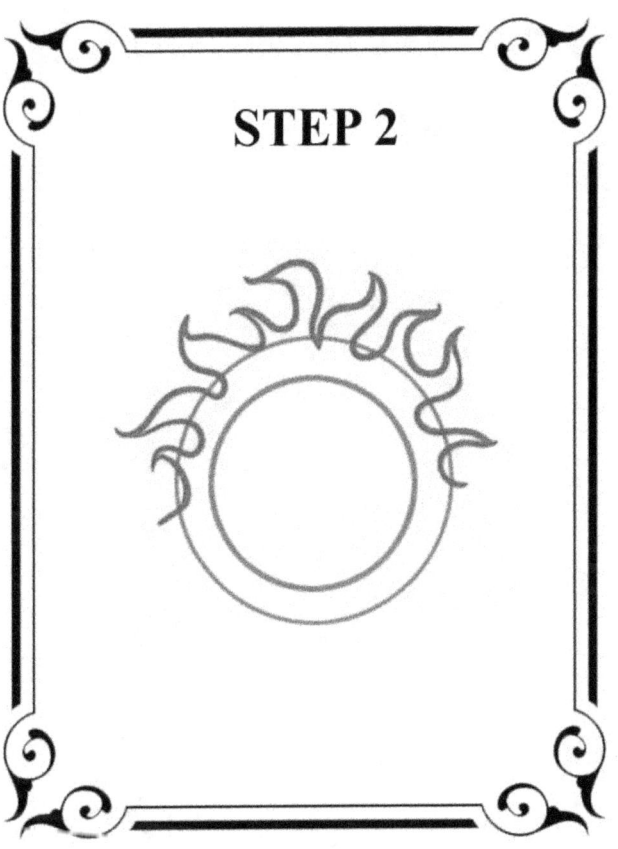

STEP 3

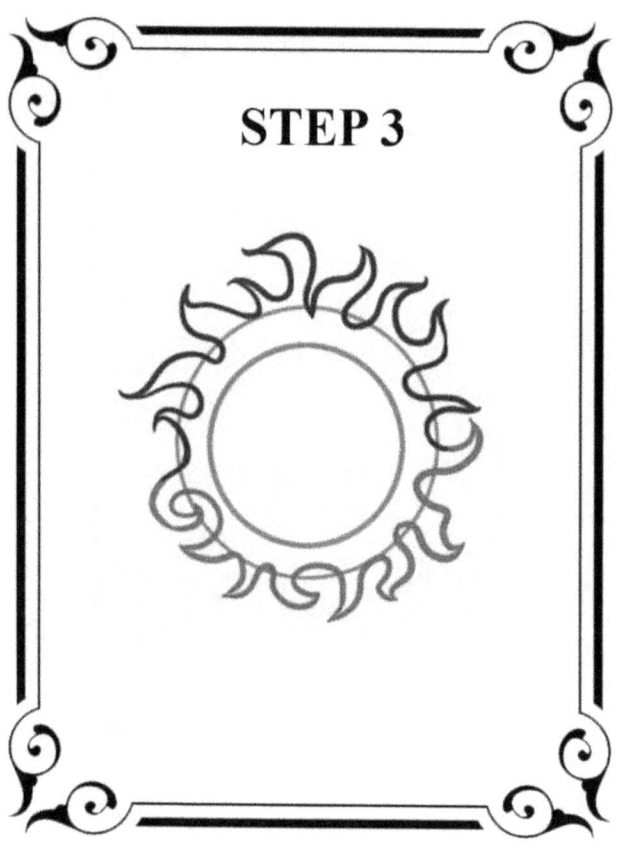

STEP 4

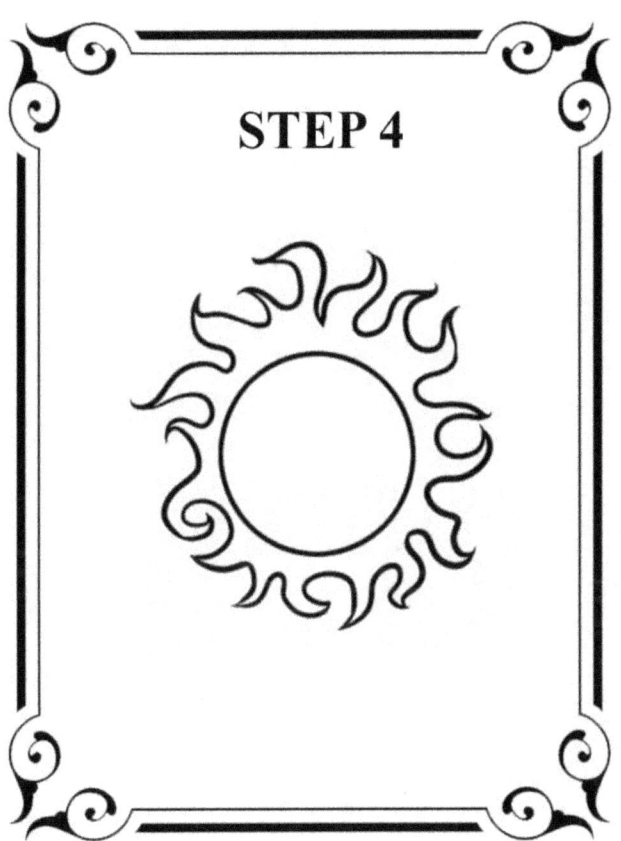